## A Message From the Publisher

CW00643181

Hello! My name is Hayden and I am
Publishing, the publishing house that br

My hope is that you and your young comedian love this book and enjoy every single page. If you do, please think about **giving us your honest feedback via a review on Amazon**. It may only take a moment, but it really does mean the world for small businesses like mine.

Even if you happen to not like this title, please let us know the reason in your review so that we may improve this title for the future and serve you better.

The mission of Hayden Fox is to create premium content for children that will help them increase their confidence and grow their imaginations while having tons of fun along the way.

Without you, however, this would not be possible, so we sincerely thank you for your purchase and for supporting our company mission.

Sincerely,
Hayden Fox

---

**GENGHIS KHAN** was tolerant of all religions. One of his interests was learning philosophical and moral lessons from other religions. Despite being a Tengrist, he often consulted with Buddhist monks, Muslims, Christian missionaries, and Taoist monks.

In Ancient Greece, wearing skirts was **MANLY.**

The first modern university was founded in Bologna, Italy in **1088.**

# FASCINATING FACTS

## FOR

# YEAR OLD KIDS

The first person to circumnavigate the world was Ferdinand **MAGELLAN,** although he did not complete the journey himself.

The first photograph ever taken was captured in **1826** by Joseph Nicéphore Niépce.

There were more than **600** plots to kill Fidel Castro.

 The first known computer programmer was a woman named Ada Lovelace who lived in the **1800S.**

The first successful airplane flight was made by the Wright Brothers in **1903.**

 The longest reigning monarch in history was Pepi II, who ruled Egypt for **94** years.

The world's oldest hotel, the Nishiyama Onsen Keiunkan, has been in operation in Japan since **705AD.**

The largest empire in history was the British Empire, which at its peak controlled nearly a **QUARTER** of the world's land and population.

The first person to reach the South Pole was Roald Amundsen in **1911.**

The first known written language was cuneiform, used in ancient Mesopotamia around 5,000 years ago.

The first successful heart transplant was performed in 1967 by Dr. Christiaan Barnard in South Africa.

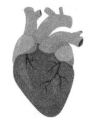

The first woman to receive a Nobel Prize was MARIE CURIE, who won the award for physics in 1903.

The oldest surviving book in the world is the Diamond Sutra, a Buddhist text printed in China in 868AD.

# WORLD WAR II involved

the majority of the world's nations, including all of the great powers, eventually forming two opposing military alliances: the Allies and the Axis.

The shortest reigning monarch in history was Louis XIX of France, who was king for only 20 MINUTES.

The World War II army of the US is the biggest army in history. Due in part to the surge of American patriotism and because of conscription, the US Army numbered **12,000,000** soldiers by the end of the war in 1945.

The **ViKiNGS** were the first people to discover America. Half a millennium before Christopher Columbus, Viking chief Leif Eriksson of Greenland landed on the Island of Newfoundland in the year 1,000 AD.

World War 2 was sparked by the invasion of Poland by **NAZi** Germany on September 1, 1939.

World War 1 was known as the **"GREAT WAR"** at the time because it was the largest and most destructive war that had ever been fought.

The Treaty of Versailles, which was signed in 1919, officially ended World War 1 and punished Germany for starting the war.

The hummingbird is the only bird that can fly **BACKWARD.**

If you were to fall into a black hole, you would experience something called **"SPAGHETTiFiCATION"** where you would be stretched out like spaghetti.

Besides Pluto, there are **FOUR** other dwarf planets in our system: Ceres, Haumea, Makemake and Eris.

There is a planet made completely out of DiAMONDS called 55 Cancri e.

ASTEROiDS can vary in size from a few meters to hundreds of kilometers.

Contrary to the movies and popular belief, the asteroid belt is fairly EASY to maneuver in a spacecraft.

Astronauts on the International Space Station see the sun rise and set 16 times a day.

FOR 11 YEAR OLDS

The earliest recorded comet is the **HALLEY** comet, which was first observed in ancient China in 239 B. C. It makes one orbit around the Sun every 75 years.

If two pieces of the same type of metal touch in space, they will permanently bond together due to a process called **COLD WELDING.**

 **ONE MILLION** Earths can fit inside the Sun.

There is a planet called KEPLER-438B that is the most Earth-like planet discovered so far and could potentially support life.

Astronauts on the moon's surface have reported a "MOON SMELL" that is described as being similar to gunpowder or burnt charcoal.

The temperature on Venus is hot enough to melt LEAD.

The HUBBLE Space Telescope has captured images of galaxies that are so far away that we are seeing them as they were billions of years ago.

There is a planet called WASP-12B that is so close to its star that its atmosphere is being stripped away by the star's gravity.

The largest moon in the solar system is GANYMEDE, which is a moon of Jupiter and is larger than the planet Mercury.

There are massive black holes that are BILLIONS of times more massive than our sun at the centers of galaxies, including our own Milky Way galaxy.

There are ROGUE planets in space that do not orbit a star and instead wander through the galaxy on their own.

The universe is thought to contain over 2 TRILLION galaxies, each with billions of stars.

One day on **VENUS** is longer than one year on Venus.

There is a planet called HD 189733b that has winds that blow at over **8,500** kilometers per hour, which is over ten times the speed of sound.

A **MANTIS SHRIMP** has the fastest punch in the animal kingdom, accelerating its claw at the speed of a bullet.

The universe is expanding at an accelerating rate, and the reason for this acceleration is thought to be due to an unknown form of energy called "DARK ENERGY"

There are GAMMA -ray bursts in space that release more energy in a few seconds than our sun will produce in its entire lifetime.

ELVIS had a black belt in Karate!

There is a phenomenon called a **"MAGNETAR,"** which is a type of neutron star with an incredibly strong magnetic field that can produce bursts of radiation that are trillions of times more powerful than an atomic bomb.

**DEER** can run up to 30 miles per hour (48 kilometers per hour).

 **RAVENS** are masters of deception.

## SEA OTTERS hold hands when they sleep so that they don't drift apart.

## PENGUiNS have a gland above their eyes that filters salt from seawater, allowing them to drink it.

## COWS have best friends.

**BUTTERFLIES** taste with their feet.

The largest flower in the world is the **RAFFLESIA,** which can grow up to three feet in diameter.

**COWS** can produce more milk when they are listening to music.

Zebra stripes act as a natural
**BUG REPELLANT.**

The breeding of lion and tigers
gives birth to off-spring known
as **LIGERS** and **TIGONS.**

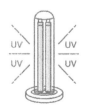

Some **BIRDS** can see
ultraviolet light, which is
invisible to humans.

A blue whale's tongue is heavier than an
**ELEPHANT.**

As opposed to other cat family members like lions and leopards who hunt at night, **CHEETAHS** are able to hunt only during the day.

A baby whale is known as a **CALF** and is cared for by the entire group.

Though fast, cheetahs
TIRE very quickly and need to
rest before they burst into
top gear again.

A **BABY SHARK** has to
fend for itself right from birth
because its mother does not
take care of it at all.

A group of rhinoceroses is
called a **CRASH.**

A **GiRAFFE'S** tongue is coated with bristly hair, which helps them to eat leaves from thorny trees like Acacia.

The average life of a dog depending on the breed can vary from **10 TO 14** years.

Elephants use their **TRUNKS** to breathe when they swim in deep waters.

The tiny pygmy marmoset is the world's smallest monkey, growing up to only **6 INCHES** long.

The common **HOUSEFLY** hums in the key of F.

Even when a snake has its eyes closed, it can still see through its EYELIDS.

The star-nosed **MOLE** can eat its body weight in worms and insects every day.

Giant Arctic jellyfish have tentacles that can reach over **36 METRES** in length.

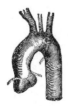 The **AORTA** is nearly the diameter of a garden hose.

The movie The Shawshank Redemption was originally a commercial **FAILURE** at the box office, but it became a beloved classic after its release on home video.

Your left lung is **SMALLER** than your right lung to make room for your heart.

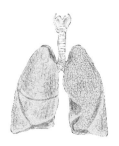

A full bladder is roughly the size of a **SOFT BALL.**

Michael Jackson's famous **MOONWALK** was inspired by a mime named Marcel Marceau and the street dance style known as the "backslide."

The speed of a **COUGH** can clock in at over 50 miles per hour (80 kilometers per hour).

About one third of humans have **20-20** vision.

The iconic
## "WHO YA GONNA CALL?" from Ghostbusters
was almost cut from the movie because the filmmakers thought it was too cheesy.

The famous "I'm king of the world!" line from TITANIC was improvised by Leonardo DiCaprio and was not in the script.

By 60 years of age, 60 percent of men and 40 percent of women will SNORE.

FOR 11 YEAR OLDS

The amount of people with perfect vision DECREASES dramatically as they age.

The hit song "All About That Bass" by Meghan Trainor was written in just **40** minutes.

 The movie The Silence of the Lambs was the first **HORROR** movie to win an Academy Award for Best Picture.

FOR 11 YEAR OLDS

The role of **NEO** in The Matrix was originally offered to Will Smith, but he turned it down to star in Wild Wild West.

Older individuals tend to lose their ability to **TASTE,** and many find that they need much more intense flavoring in order to fully appreciate a dish.

Over **90%** of diseases are caused or complicated by stress.

The "Wakanda Forever" salute from Black Panther was inspired by a gesture used by the XHOSA people of South Africa.

The role of "Tony Stark" in Iron Man was almost played by Tom Cruise, but the filmmakers decided he was TOO EXPENSIVE.

The ancient city of TROY, which was thought to be a mythical place, was discovered by a German archaeologist in the late 19th century.

The song "Hallelujah" by Leonard Cohen has been covered by over **300** different artists, making it one of the most well-covered songs in history.

The **HARRY POTTER** books were almost published under the pen name "Kenneth Grahame," a nod to the author of The Wind in the Willows.

Humans can go longer without food than **SLEEP.**

The **AZTEC** Empire, which was one of the largest and most powerful empires in the Americas, was conquered by the Spanish in the early 16th century.

James Earl Jones, the actor who voiced Darth Vader in the original Star Wars trilogy, did not initially receive **CREDIT** for the role in the movies' credits.

The **"BLACK DEATH,"** which was one of the deadliest pandemics in human history, is estimated to have killed up to 200 million people worldwide in the 14th century.

**OCTOPUSES** have three hearts and blue blood.

The tallest building in the world, the **BURJ KHALIFA** in Dubai, is more than 2 times taller than the Empire State Building.

The world's largest spider is the **GOLIATH** bird-eating spider, which can grow up to 11 inches in size.

The world's largest land animal is the **AFRICAN ELEPHANT,** which can weigh up to 13,000 pounds.

Saturn's surface is less dense than water. That means it could float in your BATHTUB, if it were big enough!

The Twitter bird's official name is LARRY.

FOR 11 YEAR OLDS

A group of pugs is called a
## GRUMBLE.

The world's largest rodent is
the **CAPYBARA,** which can
grow up to 4 feet long and
weigh up to 140 pounds.

Did you know that
**JELLYFISH** have been
around even before
dinosaurs?

Your brain generates enough electricity to power a **LIGHTBULB.**

The world's largest reptile is the saltwater crocodile, which can grow up to 23 feet long and weigh up to **2,200 POUNDS.**

There are over **9,000** benches in Central Park.

FOR 11 YEAR OLDS

The world's largest waterfall system is located in the **AMAZON** rainforest and is called the Amazon River Basin.

The world's smallest reptile is a **CHAMELEON** that can fit on a match head.

The White House has **35** bathrooms.

A **MANTIS SHRIMP** can punch with the force of a .22 caliber bullet.

How do you tell if a cranberry is ripe? It'll **BOUNCE** like a rubber ball.

Elmer Fudd's original name was EGGHEAD.

FOR 11 YEAR OLDS

In some Harry Potter movie scenes where Harry, Ron, and Hermione are doing their Hogwarts schoolwork, the actors were actually doing their **REAL** schoolwork!

The world's largest known diamond is the **CULLINAN** Diamond, which was discovered in South Africa and weighed over 3,000 carats.

The **SHORTEST** sentence in English that contains all the letters of the alphabet is "The quick brown fox jumps over a lazy dog."

# BUZZ LiGHTYEAR'S
original name was Lunar Larry.

The iconic "D'oh!" catchphrase from THE SiMPSONS was added to the show by Dan Castellaneta, the voice actor who plays Homer Simpson. It was not originally written in the script.

There is only one country on earth without mosquitoes: **ICELAND.**

FOR 11 YEAR OLDS

Marilyn Monroe's famous white dress from The Seven Year Itch was sold at auction for over **$5 MILLION** in 2011.

Snowflakes falling at 2-4 miles per hour (3-6 kilometers per hour) can take up to **ONE HOUR** to reach the ground.

The **WIND** doesn't make a sound until it blows against an object.

The word **"HURRICANE"** comes from the Taino word "huricán," who was the Carib Indian god of evil.

**TORNADOES** can form so quickly that scientists have a hard time predicting them more than a few minutes in advance.

Contrary to the popular saying, LIGHTNING often does strike the same place twice.

**LIGHTNING** can travel through the air at a speed of up to 136,000 miles per hour (219,000 kilometers per hour).

**WATERSPOUTS** can make sea creatures "rain" from the sky.

An earthquake in December **1811** caused parts of the Mississippi River to flow backward.

A **MUDSLIDE** can carry rocks, trees, vehicles and entire buildings with it!

A **HURRICANE** in Florida, USA, once caused 900 captive pythons to escape.

 The largest SNOWFLAKE ever recorded was 15 inches wide and 8 inches thick.

**THUNDERSNOW** is the name given when lightning and thunder are present in the snowstorm.

The snowiest city on Earth is AOMORI, Japan, with an average of 26 feet (8 meters) of snow each year.

The ocean contains enough salt to cover all the continents to a height of nearly 500 FEET.

The temperature in the Earth's core is estimated to be around **6,000** degrees Celsius, which is hotter than the surface of the sun.

The Northern Lights, or **AURORA BOREALIS,** are caused by solar particles colliding with Earth's atmosphere and can create beautiful light displays in the night sky.

The driest place on Earth is the ATACAMA Desert in Chile, where some areas have not received rain in over 500 years.

The world's largest temperature range in a single day was recorded in LOMA, Montana, where the temperature went from –54°F to 49°F in less than 24 hours.

In 525BC, a sandstorm buried hundreds of soldiers in an Egyptian desert.

BLACK iCE, a transparent coating of ice on a surface, can make pavements super-slippery but is hard to see.

A 26-sided shape is known as a rhombicuboctahedron.

A group of lemurs is called a
## CONSPIRACY.

CAPTIVE tigers in the U.S. alone outnumber the number of wild tigers worldwide.

**FACEBOOK** will track and record nearly everything you do if you browse the web while logged in to your Facebook account..

Albert Einstein had mastered calculus by the tender age of **15.**

Madagascar's name was first seen in the memoirs of the 13th century Italian explorer, **MARCO POLO.**

The longest Cricket Test match lasted 12 days between England and South Africa. It had to be ended in a draw because otherwise the English team would have missed their boat home.

The tall chef's hat is called a
## TOQUE BLANCHE.

The average person will spend SIX MONTHS of their life waiting for red traffic lights to turn green.

The **LONGEST** name in the world for a place is Taumatawhakatangihangakoauau otamateaturipukakapikimaungaho ronukupokaiwhenuakitanatahu, which is a hill in New Zealand.

The first-ever documented feature film was made in Australia in **1906.**

When dogs are first born, they are completely **BLiND** & cannot hear anything. The first senses which they develop are the senses of smell touch.

**JUSTIN BiEBER'S** first tweet was in March 2009.

The original name for Xbox was **DiRECTX BOX.**

 The shortest commercial flight in the world is between the Scottish islands of Westray and Papa Westray. The distance is only **1.7 MiLES** and takes less than two minutes.

In Switzerland, it is ILLEGAL to own just one guinea pig. This is because guinea pigs are social animals, and they are considered victims of abuse if they are alone.

The world's largest bicycle parking lot is located in Utrecht, Netherlands, and can hold over **12,500** bicycles.

Every 10 years, the human skeleton **REPAIRS** and renews itself. Essentially, you have different bones now than you did 10 years ago!

Abraham Lincoln loved CATS and once let one eat from the table during a formal White House dinner.

There are over 1,000 different species of bamboo in the world.

You can now get a headstone with a QR CODE. Called "Living Headstones", they show pages with photos, video biographies, and comments from loved ones.

## DANiEL RADCLiFFE

had the same stunt double for the first six Harry Potter movies. Unfortunately, he became paralyzed after an on-set accident.

An adult's kidney weighs about 160 grams and is the size of a
## FiST.

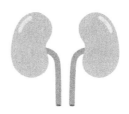

There is a city in Turkey called
## BATMAN.

 There are over **7,500** varieties of apples grown around the world.

Potatoes are made of **80%** water.

 There are **15 BiLLiON** jelly beans eaten every year.

**CHOCOLATE** was used as currency by the ancient Mayans and Aztecs.

**SUBWAY** was sued for selling footlongs that were less than a foot long.

 In the future, your meat might come from a **BIOTECH LAB,** not a farm.

It takes **660** gallons of water to make one hamburger.

**BABY CARROTS** are just adult carrots that have been shaved down to smaller sizes.

The five-second rule is **FALSE.**

**ORANGES** aren't always orange in color.

**POPCORN** was first discovered in Mexico over 9,000 years ago.

The world's oldest chocolate bar is over **100** years old.

Pineapples take 2 YEARS to grow!

CANNED PEACHES are the first fruit to ever be consumed on the moon.

Peanuts are not actually nuts - they are LEGUMES.

FOR 11 YEAR OLDS

The largest piece of cheese ever made weighed over 34,000 pounds.

POPSICLES were invented by a child named Frank Epperson in 1905.

 STRAWBERRIES are the only fruit with seeds on the outside.

The DURIAN fruit is so smelly that it's banned in some public places in Southeast Asia.

A strawberry isn't actually a BERRY, but a banana is.

There's a black market for certain high-end CHEESES.

The world's largest vegetable is the **PUMPKIN.**

**VANiLLA** comes from the seed pods of a type of orchid.

McDonald's sells **75** burgers every second.

Wheelchair tennis legend, Esther Vergeer, retired after **470** - straight wins and four Paralympic golds.

Michael Jordan, Bo Jackson, and Wayne Gretzky starred in a short-lived 1991 NBC Saturday morning cartoon called PRO STARS.

The shortest boxing match in history lasted only **11** seconds.

 The OLYMPIC FLAME is lit using a parabolic mirror to focus the sun's rays.

China did not win an Olympic medal until **1952**.

The tradition of fans doing the wave at sports events started in Mexico City during the **1986** World Cup.

Only 72 players in NBA history have attempted more free throws in their careers than the 5,317 Shaquille O'Neal missed.

The phrase about winning something "HANDS DOWN" originally referred to a jockey who won a race without whipping his horse or pulling back the reins.

The fastest ever recorded tennis serve was hit by Sam Groth in 2012 and traveled at a speed of 163.7 mph.

**LiCHTENSTEIN** has competed in the most Summer Olympics without winning any medal.

The sport of squash was invented in the United Kingdom in the **1830S.**

The longest tennis match in history lasted **11 HOURS AND 5 MiNUTES.**

In professional **SUMO** wrestling in Japan, if a wrestler steps out of the ring or touches the ground with any part of his body other than the soles of his feet, he loses the match.

The oldest golf course in the world is the Old Course at St Andrews in Scotland, which has been in use since the **1400S.**

The **STANLEY CUP,** awarded to the winners of the NHL playoffs, is the oldest professional sports trophy in North America.

The first golf balls were made
of **WOOD.**

The tallest NBA player in history
# GHEORGHE MURESAN,
was 7 feet 7 inches tall.

In 1937, **CHEETAHS** were
raced at Romford Greyhound
Stadium in an effort to
increase attendance.

The first Olympic Games to feature women's events was the 1900 **PARiS OLYMPiCS.**

The first modern Olympic Games were held in Athens, Greece in **1896.**

Major League Baseball teams use about **850,000** balls per season.

In **1898**, one of the first programs to be broadcast on radio was a yacht race that took place in British waters.

The first game of **BASKETBALL** was played with a soccer ball and two peach baskets.

**BASEBALL** was invented in the United States in the early 19th century.

The highest score ever recorded in a professional American football game was 222–0 between the Cumberland College Bulldogs and the Georgia Tech Engineers in **1916.**

The World Wide Web was coined by Tim Berners-Lee in **1990.**

The first website ever created is still online. It was created by Tim Berners-Lee, the inventor of the WORLD WIDE WEB.

Although the public had access to the internet in the 1980s, it did not become widely accessible until the **1990S.**

The term **'SURFiNG'** the internet was coined by blogger Net Mom in 1992.

**AOL** used half of all CD-ROM discs in the 1990s.

The "@" symbol used in email addresses was originally used to denote "at the rate of."

The first social media platform was Six Degrees, launched in 1997.

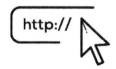 The world's first website was hosted on a NEXT computer.

Today's social media feeds have RSS technology to thank.

The first YouTube video was uploaded in 2005 and showed one of the co-founders at the zoo.

 The first BITCOIN transaction happened in 2009.

**CRYPTOCURRENCY** is a type of digital or virtual money that uses cryptography to secure and verify transactions.

Up to **20%** of Google searches were brand new in 2012.

The first cryptocurrency, Bitcoin, was created in **2009** by an unknown person or group using the pseudonym Satoshi Nakamoto.

A single Google query uses
**1,000** computers.

Cryptocurrencies are
DECENTRALIZED, which
means they are not controlled
by any government or central
authority.

The most expensive keyword
for Google Adwords is
**"iNSURANCE".**

**WEB3** is a new version of the internet that is focused on decentralization and allowing users to have more control over their data and online activities.

The first **TWEET** was sent on March 21, 2006.

The world record for fastest time to log into Gmail is **1.16** seconds.

The AMAZON logo indicates you can get everything from A to Z.

BLOCKCHAIN is the technology that underlies most cryptocurrencies and is used to securely store and record transactions.

The weight of the internet is estimated to be about

## 50 GRAMS.

The supply of many cryptocurrencies is **LIMITED,** meaning there is a set amount that will ever be created.

**ETHEREUM** is the second-largest cryptocurrency and is known for its ability to support smart contracts, which are self-executing contracts with the terms of the agreement between buyer and seller being directly written into lines of code.

**CRYPTOCURRENCIES**

can be bought and sold on specialized exchanges or through peer-to-peer networks.

Cryptocurrencies can be stored in DiGiTAL wallets, which are software programs that allow users to securely store, send, and receive cryptocurrencies.

EBAY once tried changing their background from yellow to white but received complaints. They reverted it to yellow, but then gradually changed it to white over several months. Nobody complained.

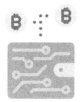

Cryptocurrency transactions can be anonymous, but they are NOT completely private or untraceable.

Chronic exposure to silver or silver dust can cause argyria. The most dramatic symptom of **ARGYRIA** is that the skin permanently turns blue or bluish-grey.

Night vision goggles use green phosphor because the human eye can differentiate more shades of **GREEN** than any other color, allowing for greater differentiation of objects in the picture.

The brief perception of **RED** prior to an important test (e.g., an IQ test) can hurt performance.

In the 1980s, a team in New York showed that an enzyme from green **COFFEE BEANS** could remove the B antigen from red blood cells. Thereby turning any blood type into group O, the universal donor.

**COLORS** are wavelengths of light that are usually perceived based on which wavelengths are absorbed or reflected by an object.

Green evokes mainly positive emotions such as relaxation and comfort because it reminds us of **NATURE.**

 An experiment by Frank Farley and Alfred Grant questioned whether color or black-and-white multimedia presentations would affect subjects' MEMORY. Their results showed that the subjects did show better memory of the colored presentations.

The painter's color wheel is DIFFERENT from the printer's color wheel.

 Judges used to dress in RED.

Some businesses are starting to **ACCEPT** cryptocurrencies as a form of payment, including Tesla, Microsoft, and AT&T.

Cryptocurrency has been used to fund various **CHARITABLE** causes, including disaster relief efforts and animal welfare organizations.

Some countries have **BANNED** or restricted the use of cryptocurrencies, including China and Russia.

**WEB3** is still in its early stages of development, and there is a lot of excitement and speculation about how it could change the internet and the way we interact with technology.

**IMPOSSIBLE** colors are colors that are too complex for the human eye.

**COLORS** can be optical illusions.

Many people believe that
# CRYPTOCURRENCIES
have the potential to revolutionize the way we think about money and financial transactions.

Colors can trigger deep childhood **MEMORIES.**

**WHITE** is the most popular car color.

Men and women see the color **RED** slightly differently.

The colors of a **RAINBOW** always appear in the same order.

**COLORS** affect our depth perception.

A cheetah can run up to 76 miles per hour (122 kilometers per hour) and can go from 0 to 68 miles per hour (109 kilometers per hour) in less than three seconds.

The GOLDEN RATIO (approximately 1.618) is a special number that appears in nature and art, and is considered to be aesthetically pleasing.

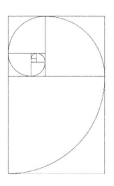

The equal sign '=' was invented by an English mathematician in 1557.

## CRYPTOCURRENCY,
such as Bitcoin, uses complex mathematical algorithms to verify and secure transactions.

## GEOMETRY is used to
design and build structures such as buildings, bridges, and roads.

## TRIGONOMETRY is used in
navigation and astronomy to calculate distances, angles, and trajectories.

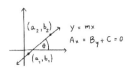

**ALGEBRA** is used in many real-life situations, such as calculating distance and time for travel, and budgeting and financial planning.

The power of exponential growth is shocking. Compound interest, which results in exponential growth, was quoted as the 8TH wonder of the world by Einstein.

A googol is a number with **100** zeros.

The study of **PROBABILITY** helps us understand risk and make informed decisions about insurance, investments, and other financial matters.

To make the perfect sugar cookie, follow a simple ratio of **3:2:1,** or 3 parts flour to 2 parts butter to 1 part sugar.

Adding up the numbers 1–100 consecutively (1+2+3+4+5...) gives you **5050.**

The **FiBONACCi** sequence is a series of numbers in which each number is the sum of the two preceding ones: 1, 1, 2, 3, 5, 8, 13, 21, 34, 55, and so on.

Over 2000 years ago, Eratosthenes estimated the Earth's circumference using math, without ever leaving Egypt, and he was accurate to within **2%.**

The number **13** is considered unlucky in many Western cultures.

The concept of INFINITY, which is used in calculus and other mathematical fields, is a fundamental part of understanding the universe and our place in it.

Computers use BINARY code (0s and 1s) to represent all data and instructions, and complex algorithms to perform calculations and solve problems.

STATISTICS is used in political polling to predict election outcomes and gauge public opinion.

If you count up the number of letters in the 13 different kinds of playing cards (ace, two, three, four, five, six, seven, eight, nine, ten, jack, queen, king) you will find that there are 52 letters, exactly the number of playing cards in a deck (excluding jokers).

There are 80,658,175,170,943,878,571,660,6 36,856, 403,766,975,289,505,440,883,27 7,824,000,000,000,000 ways to arrange a **PACK OF CARDS.**

The first pair of scissors were invented in ancient Egypt around 1500 BC.

The concept of ZERO, which was developed in ancient India, revolutionized mathematics and paved the way for modern algebra and calculus.

GAME theory, which uses mathematical models to predict outcomes in strategic situations, is used in economics, politics, and military strategy.

The largest named number is a GOOGOLPLEX, which is 10 to the power of a googol (10^100).

The first working telephone was invented by Alexander Graham Bell in 1876. His famous first words spoken over the phone were, "Mr. Watson, come here, I want to see you."

The **TALLEST** man in recorded history was Robert Wadlow, who was 8 feet, 11 inches tall.

CLEOPATRA lived closer in time to the invention of the iPhone than to the construction of the Great Pyramid of Giza.

A "SUNDOG" is a type of atmospheric phenomenon that creates bright spots of light on either side of the sun.

The "EYE of the Hurricane" is a calm area in the center of a hurricane that can be as much as 20 miles wide.

The world's largest tornado outbreak occurred in 2011 when over 350 tornadoes hit the United States in just four days.

FOR 11 YEAR OLDS

The SUN is the most important source of energy for Earth. It generates weather patterns, provides the energy plants need so that they can grow, and provides the oxygen and food that we need to survive!

If the sun was to suddenly disappear, we wouldn't notice for another EIGHT minutes as this is how long it takes sunlight to reach Earth.

Some of the windiest places on Earth can be found in Midwest America – Chicago is even known as The WINDY CITY.

## Leave Your Feedback on Amazon

Please think about leaving some feedback via a review on Amazon. It may only take a moment, but it really does mean the world for small businesses like mine.

Even if you did not enjoy this title, please let us know the reason(s) in your review so that we may improve this title and serve you better.

## From the Publisher

Hayden Fox's mission is to create premium content for children that will help them expand their vocabulary, grow their imaginations, gain confidence, and share tons of laughs along the way.

Without you, however, this would not be possible, so we sincerely thank you for your purchase and for supporting our company mission.

Printed in Great Britain
by Amazon